Colorplan
Cobalt
135 gsm
from G.F Smith

Portrait of a Company

Strathmore
Pastelle
Natural White
118 gsm
from G.F Smith

Foreword

G.F Smith is a company rich with stories, full of characters as varied and distinct as the papers in its collection. Its long history is one of sustained and successful growth, and it takes pride in being an independent British company that has taken skills, expertise and paper to the rest of the world.

It continues to develop and grow, doing business in the same spirit as its founder, George Frederick Smith, by listening to customers and then setting about meeting their needs. Today, as the masters of our own destiny we are able to do things differently, as our loyal customers would no doubt testify. It means we can offer an almost unparalleled level of personal service, based on decades of experience, generations of craftsmanship and a constant desire to learn and improve every aspect of what we do.

As George Frederick Smith began his journey, and the company discovered new papers in new lands, so we too continue to experiment, seeking new and beautiful papers, pioneering new techniques, and finding better ways to serve our customers.

People are our foundation, but paper is our passion, and it is this, above all else, that defines G.F Smith.

G . F SMITH

1885 ONWARDS

George Frederick Smith's guiding passion was a love of paper and a fascination for its limitless possibilities. This singular obsession led him to establish G.F Smith & Son in 1885. He found premises, equipment and hard working employees. He won loyal customers in the printing, publishing and commercial arts. Most importantly, he sought out and gathered supplies of beautiful paper. His passion took the business across the Atlantic, forming bonds that stay strong to this day. By land and sea he brought these papers back home.

Step by step with his son by his side, he listened to the needs of his customers and set about delivering them. Over time, his company grew to become part of the fabric of Hull and today, from its factory at the heart of the city, G.F Smith thrives, supplying exceptional papers to customers all over the world. The business is still founded on his principles of loyalty and respect, hard work and fair reward, and an admiration for the creative spirit that is embodied by the designers that turn to us for the papers that help bring their ideas to life. Most importantly, G.F Smith retains a love for and obsession with paper.

Today, more than ever, paper's simple beauty has re-asserted its importance in our lives. In a world of transient communication and fleeting digital memories, paper offers texture and feeling, weight and sensation. Paper reminds us that skill, craft and creativity coupled with something as naturally beautiful as paper can leave a lasting and powerful impression.

It is our intention to serve our customers with the same passion and pride that George Frederick did nearly 130 years ago. And it is our privilege to be custodians of what he established. We will do everything we can to make sure his legacy continues long after our own time at G.F Smith has ended.

Finally, we must thank the Directors past and present who have guided the company with such vision and ambition. And we must thank the staff, whose hard work, loyalty and commitment from 1885 onwards has been central to our growth, our continued success and our enviable reputation.

Sincerely,

John Haslam
Joint Managing Director

Phil Alexander
Joint Managing Director

Lockwood Street, Hull HU2 0HL
Six Bridges Trading Estate, Marlborough Grove, London SE1 5JT

Portrait of a Company

Portrait of a Company

Our Story
Our People
Our Work

Our Story

Zen
Pure White
150 gsm
from G.F Smith

Photographed on Strathmore Grandee Natural from G.F Smith

1885

George Frederick Smith Establishes G.F Smith

After spending his early working life as a commercial traveller, selling paper and stationery to printers and publishers, at 51 years of age, George Frederick Smith moves from Manchester to London to set up a company as a paper merchant. In partnership with his eldest son Thomas Brooks Smith, they establish G.F Smith to source, supply and sell paper. As demand grows, George and Thomas begin sourcing specialised papers from mills in Britain, Europe and America.

The Smith Family

An early family photograph of George Frederick Smith (fourth from left) and Thomas Brooks Smith (sixth from left) at the wedding of Horatio Nelson Smith, George's youngest son, to Margaret Syme.

```
                                                    Feb.2nd.,1900.
G.F.Smith & Son,
        Trafalgar Buildings,
Gentlemen:----          Charing Cross, London, W.C.
        In reply to yours of Jan.16th.:-
                        We have not changed our minds
about placing our goods with you as soon as we are able to deliver. We
have delayed replying in the hope of being able to be more definite in
regard to the time when we can deliver our goods. This will probably be not
before the first of July. We certainly hope to meet your views and trust
that our relations may be advantageous to you as well as to ourselves.
        It is quite likely that you have heard from Mr Moses, as I understand
he proposes to make you his agents. I think that if you will get into com-
munication with Eaton, Dykeman & Co., South Lee, Massachusetts, U.S.A., that
you can make advantageous arrangements for blotters. I have written to Mr
Eaton, a personal friend of mine, to send you samples.
                With kind regards and best wishes, I am,
                        Yours Truly,
                                The B.D.Rising Paper Co.
```

1899

A Visit to Strathmore Paper Mill

Thomas Brooks Smith (pictured right) travels by boat to North America in an attempt to source papers from the Strathmore Paper Mill. Thomas finds it almost impossible to meet with the mill's founder, Horace Moses, and decides to visit him at home, unannounced, on a Saturday. The visit is not going well, that is until Mrs Moses arrives at the house in a state of panic. The organist due to play at church that day has been taken ill. Thomas, an accomplished pianist, steps in. The Moses family are so impressed with the impromptu recital that they have Thomas's luggage brought from the local hotel and insist he spends the rest of his stay as their house guest. Quite apart from earning the respect of Moses, Thomas's offer of help is the catalyst to a lasting partnership between the two companies. In 1900, G.F Smith becomes the exclusive merchant for Strathmore throughout Britain and mainland Europe.

1900

The Search for Papers Continues

Though constantly seeking out new papers in Britain and Europe, Thomas's first trip to America continues to pay dividends. The letter shown above (one of the earliest in the archives that survived damage in wartime) is from Bradley D. Rising, the proprietor of Rising Paper Company. It confirms an order for blotting paper to be delivered to G.F Smith in July 1900. Blotting paper was in regular use right up until the middle of the 20th century, thanks to the use of long-hand writing and dipping pens.

1904

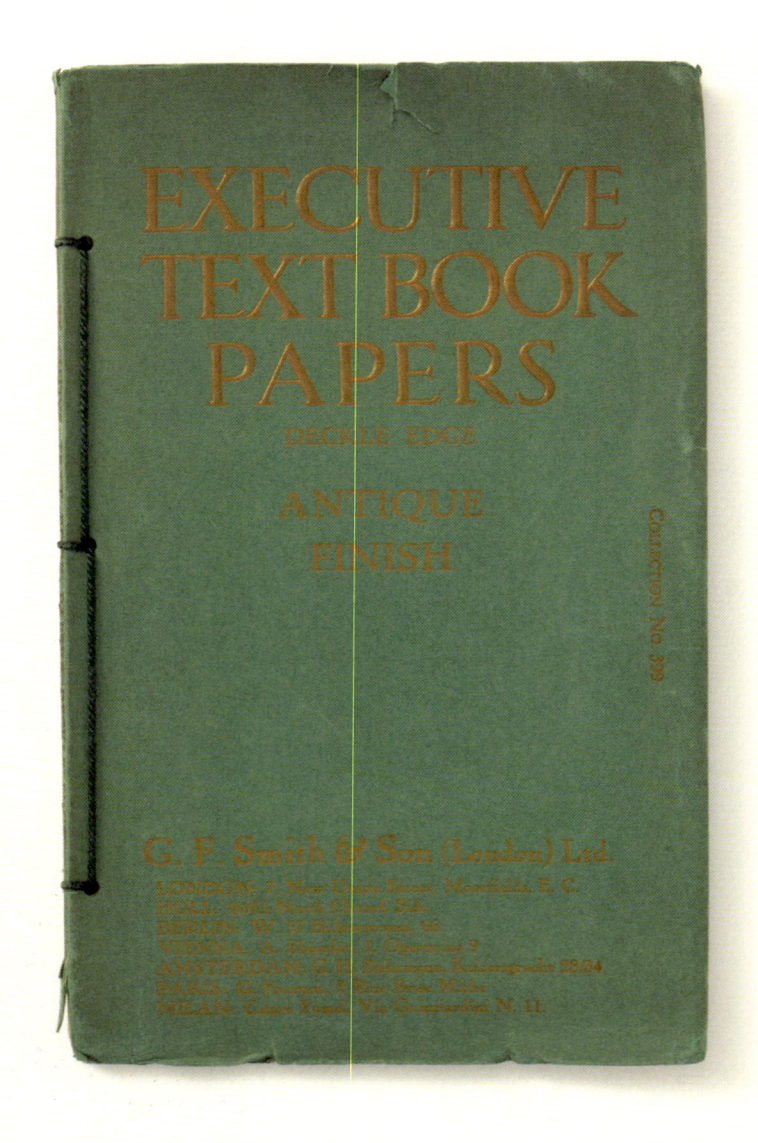

G.F Smith Becomes a Limited Company

1905

An 18-year-old named Herbert Thomlinson starts work at the company as a Sales Clerk. He will soon play a very significant role in the future of G.F Smith.

1909

Strathmore Executive Text Book Papers Sample Book

Just one of the many sample books produced by Strathmore at the turn of the century. All sample books at this time contain examples of various applications in commercial print aimed to educate, inspire and encourage printers to use Strathmore Coloured and Textured Papers and Boards. Strathmore is the first paper mill in the world to produce sample books containing examples of commercial print along with a swatch style presentation.

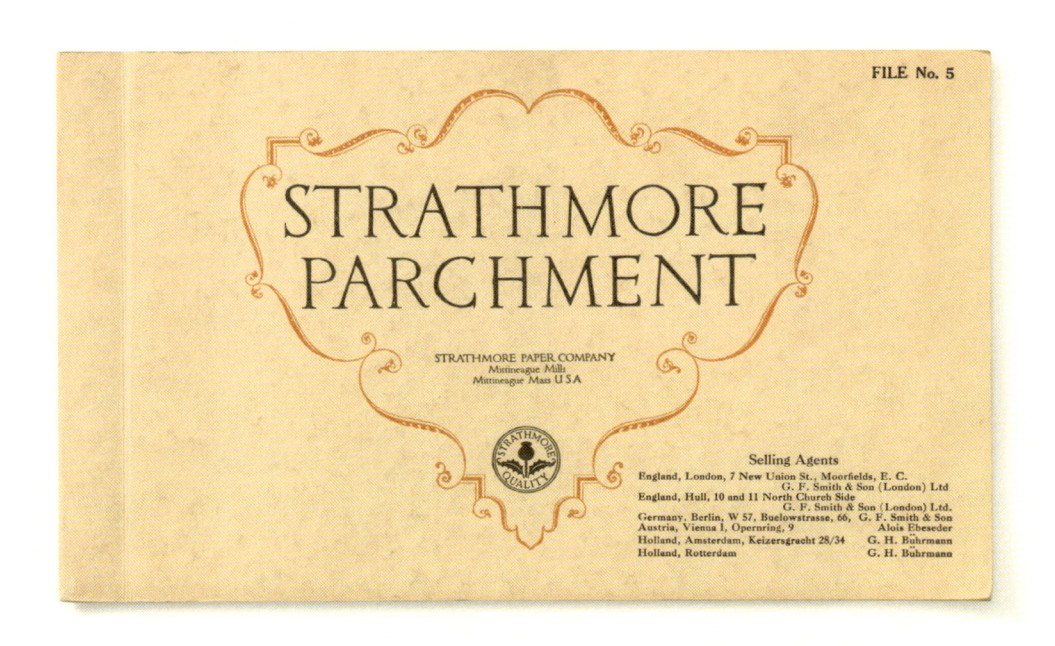

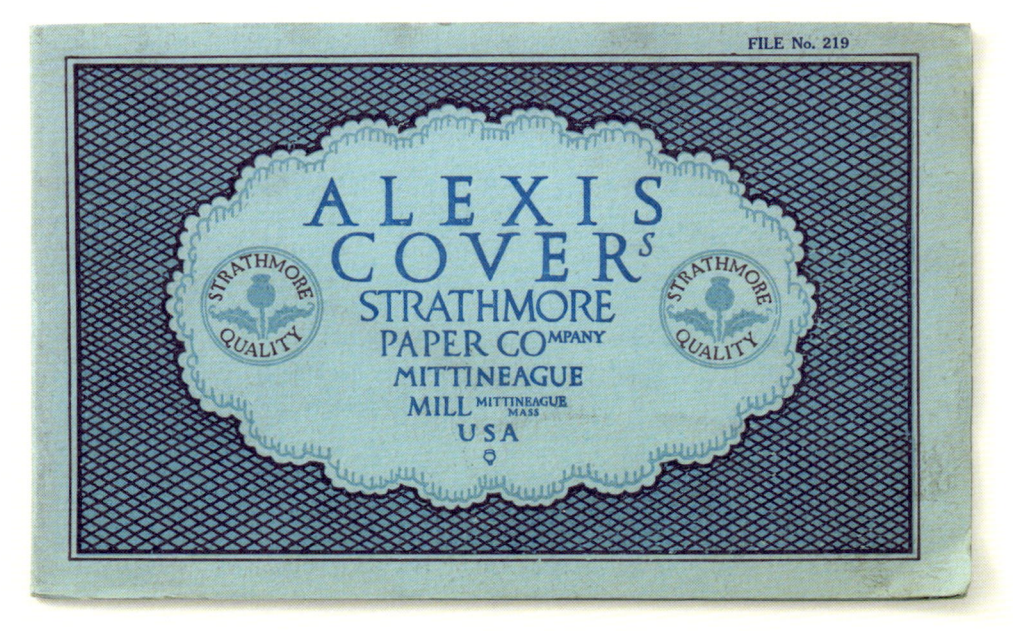

1912-15

Strathmore Sample Books and Promotions

These sample books are used to sell Strathmore Paper Mill products, imported by G.F Smith, to customers in Britain, France, Germany, Austria, Italy and Holland.

1915

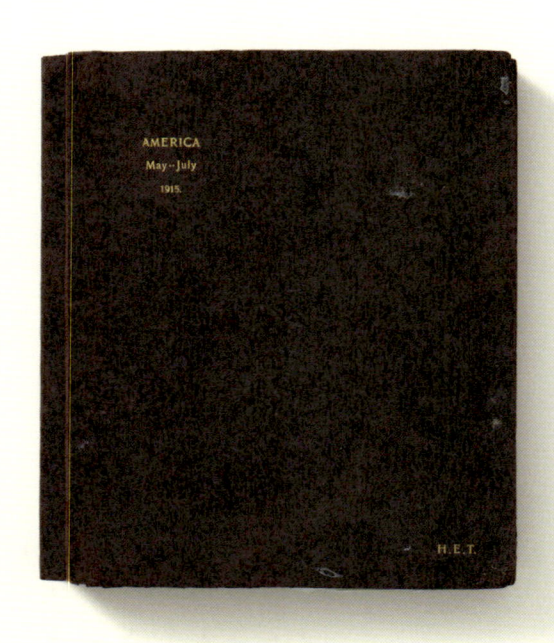

Mr Thomlinson Travels to America

Despite the impact of the war, Strathmore Paper Mill is confident enough in the ability of G.F Smith to recover that it takes ownership of the company and writes off the debt. Mr Thomlinson travels to West Springfield in Massachusetts via New York to agree the deal. The photographs shown above are from Mr Thomlinson's own photo album (shown wearing the bowler hat), recording his trip across the Atlantic and his time in North America.

1914

Debt Threatens the Business

As the First World War rages, all of the Strathmore stocks held by G.F Smith's agents in mainland Europe are either impounded or destroyed. As a result, the company falls into debt with Strathmore, still the owner of all the paper that has been lost.

1916

A New Marketing Strategy

Mr Thomlinson returns from Strathmore Paper Mill inspired by the mill, its products, its people and its revolutionary marketing and promotional work. He introduces direct mail campaigns, starting with the development of a mailing list of existing and potential customers. To build the list, a student from a commercial college in Hull, Miss Beatrice Harrison, is brought into G.F Smith on secondment. Mr Thomlinson is so impressed with her efforts that he offers Miss Harrison a job as a book-keeper the moment her studies are complete. She will spend the rest of her working life at G.F Smith, becoming Company Secretary in 1947 and a Director of the business in 1949, a position she held until her retirement in 1958.

1918

The photograph above shows London staff enjoying the sea air on an away day.

Mr Thomlinson takes over from Thomas Brooks Smith and is appointed as Managing Director.

1926

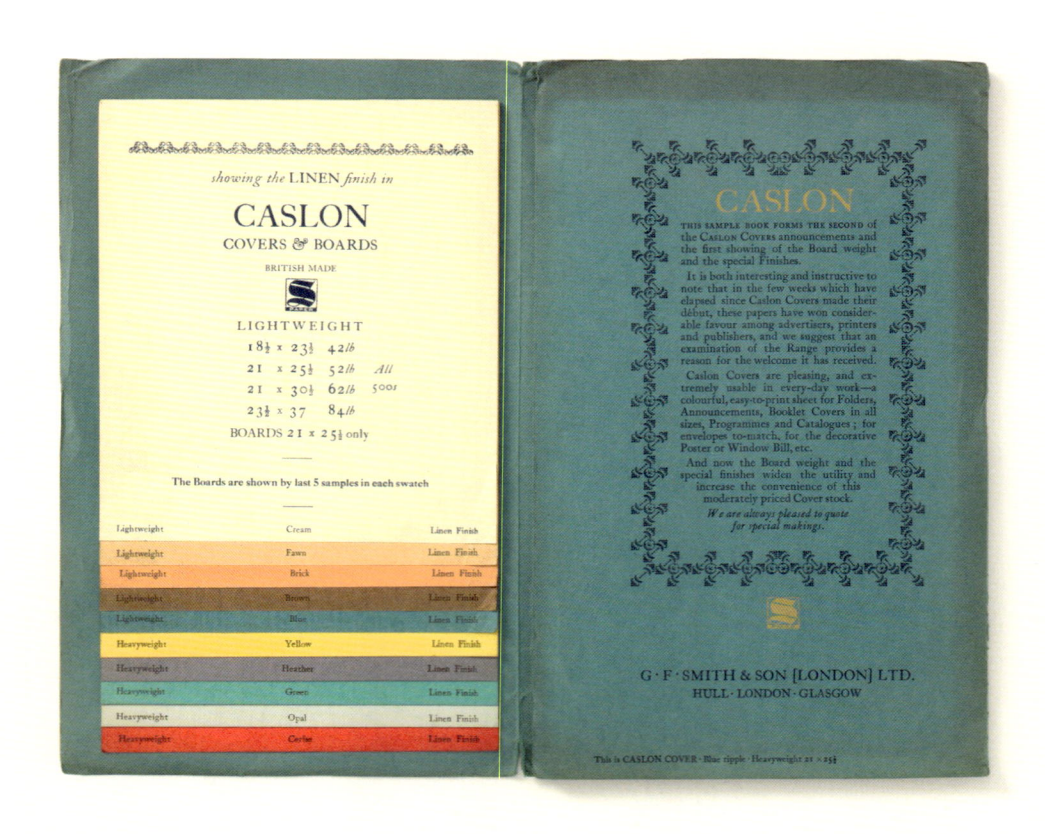

Release of the Caslon Covers & Boards Sample Book

The company starts trading with Scottish paper mill Robert Craig & Son, specialists in the production of coloured and embossed papers and boards at their mill in Airdrie. They manufacture a series of ranges exclusively for G.F Smith, using reel and sheet fed embossing machines to enhance the product.
The first of these exclusive ranges is launched under the name 'Caslon Covers' and includes ten colours in both paper and board weights, supplied in Antique, Linen and Ripple embossed textures. Craig's continue to be G.F Smith's principle supplier of cover paper and boards until the mill's closure in 1972.

1935

Release of the Cumberland Covers Sample Book

Such had been the success of the embossed Cover Paper range produced by Robert Craig that in 1932 Mr Thomlinson incorporates a factory into the Osborne Street site in Hull. He installs guillotines, embossers and duplexing machines. These services add flexibility, diversification and improved quality and service to customers. This is followed, in 1935, by the introduction of a department specialising in the production of hand-made envelopes. G.F Smith can now take orders for a minimum of 200 envelopes in four different styles in any size made from any of the cover papers offered in the various ranges. This new service is featured in every subsequent sample book.

1939

Supplies are Restricted

The outbreak of the Second World War dramatically reduces the supply of paper from British and American mills. Many G.F Smith staff leave their positions to enlist or to take work in engineering and munitions in Hull. Many will return to their role once the war is over.

Photographed on Colorplan China White from G.F Smith

1941

Bombs Fall on Hull

On the night of 8 May 1941 German aircraft drop 157 tonnes of high explosive and 20,000 incendiary bombs onto the city of Hull. 116 people are killed and 160 more are seriously injured. The Osborne Street site, with its machinery, stocks and the company archive is reduced to rubble. By a miracle there are no casualties. Within 48 hours enemy bombs completely demolish G.F Smith's office on Turnmill Street in London.

G·F·SMITH & SON
(LONDON) LIMITED

Paper Merchants

TEMPORARY ADDRESS:
NATIONAL PROVINCIAL BANK CHAMBERS · SILVER STREET · HULL

14 MAY 1941

Dear Sirs,

We regret to have to inform you that our stocks, plant and machinery—at both this and our London Warehouses, have been completely destroyed by enemy action, during the past week.

We have certain stocks available at our mills, from which we shall be able to give you some service—meanwhile may we ask for your support and co-operation, until such time as we are again in a position to resume production ourselves.

Yours faithfully,

G. F. SMITH & SON (Hull) LTD.

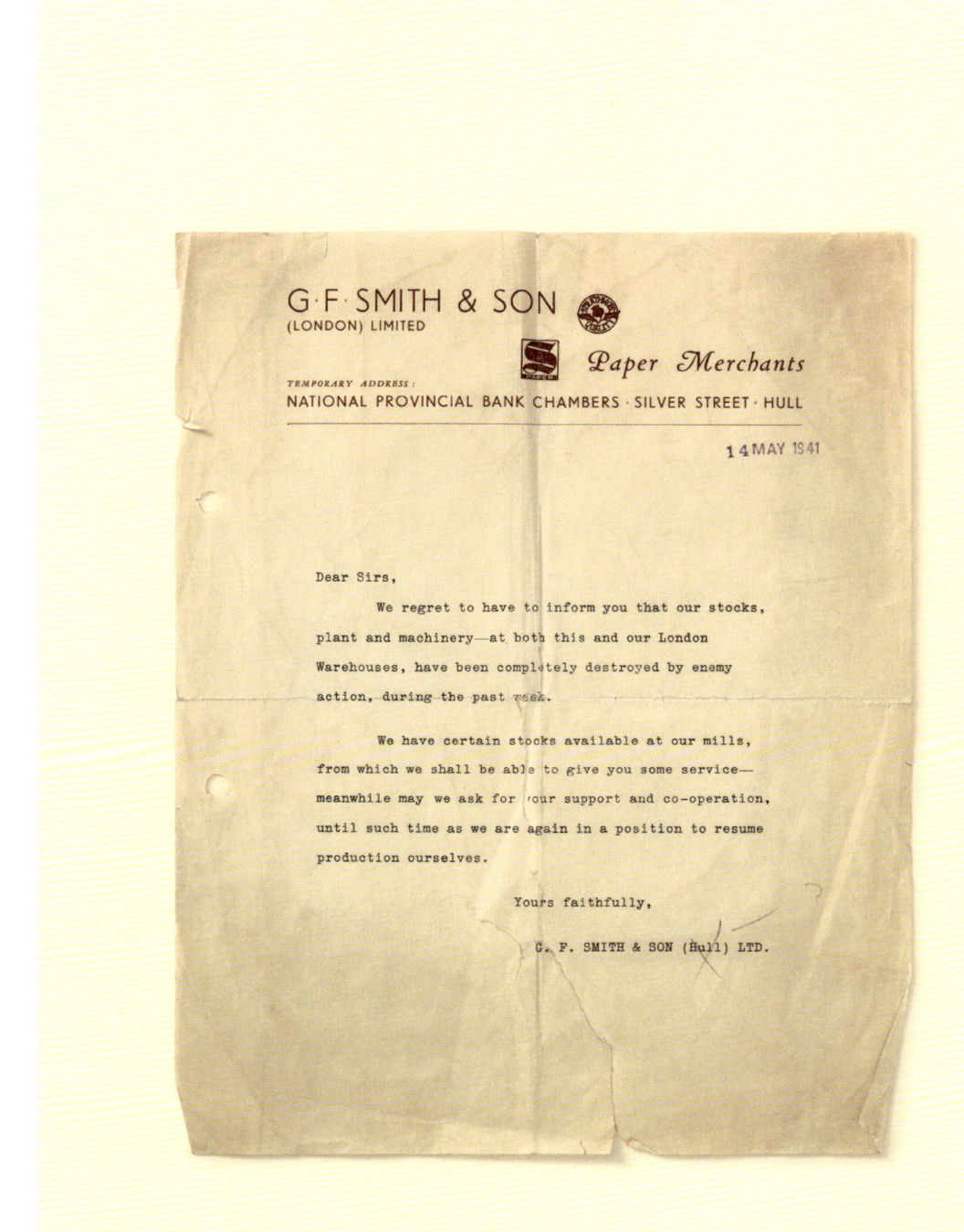

Disruption of Services

The stock, machinery and records at G.F Smith's Hull and London offices are all but destroyed in German bombing raids. On 14 May 1941 the company writes to all its customers and suppliers outlining the impact of the bombings on day-to-day operations. Within days the two offices are back up and running. The Hull staff relocates to a large house with a garage and outbuildings in the city's Avenue district and in London, the staff move to the Area Manager's home in Hertford for the remainder of the war. Staff in both offices work tirelessly in far from ideal conditions to keep the business going, ready to rebuild when the war is over. Their drive and determination remain key parts of the ethos of the business.

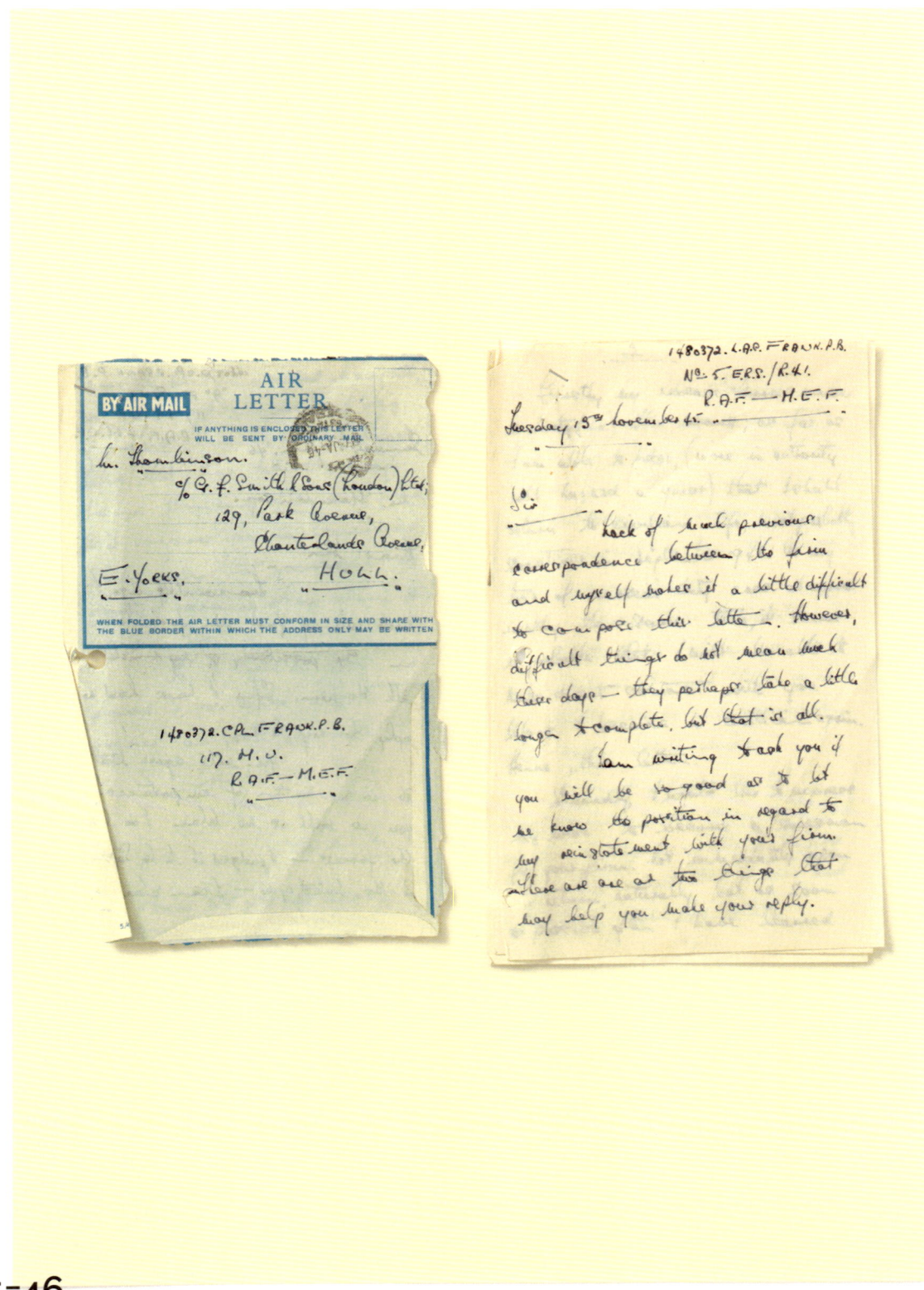

1945–46

Return and Re-employment

Having joined the company as an office boy, Peter Basil Frank enlisted to serve in the RAF at the outbreak of the war. On 15 November 1945, Peter Frank writes to Mr Thomlinson from overseas asking if he might be re-instated on his return.

January
Eighteenth
1946

Cpl. P.B. Frank, 1480372
M.E.F.

Dear Frank,

This is to acknowledge your letter of the 5th. It is more than difficult to write and tell you just what I would like to do - in view of the difficulties we are up against in HULL.

Actually the situation with regard to ourselves is very little changed from 1941. While we have at long last managed to secure a very old building, we have not yet obtained licence to alter it to suit ourselves and are hardly likely to obtain such licence for some considerable time.

It will, I should say, be another 12 months before we are able to occupy our new building. After that everything depends upon the amount of raw material which will be allowed us by the Paper Control- and as you will see it is very difficult for me to say just how and when we shall be able to re-instate you.

As a matter of fact there are about eight of our former employees in the same position as yourself and so far for two of them only have I been able to find jobs. Others I am advising to look for jobs elsewhere if only temporary ones.

Of course, things may be changed by the time you obtain your release and I certainly hope they will.

Whether or not I would, under favourable circumstances, be able to offer you a job on the sales side I cannot promise but by all means, in your own interests, take up the course of Salesmanship to which you refer.

Best Wishes to you,

Sincerely yours,

On 18 January 1946, Mr Thomlinson replies stating that the company is still in recovery and working from temporary premises. Unable to give an assurance of re-employment, he promises that as soon as the situation improves he will get back in touch. In March 1946, following his de-mobilisation, Peter Frank is appointed to the position of Sales Clerk in Hull, just months before the business moves to Lockwood Street.

In 1962, Peter Frank was made Sales Director, then appointed Managing Director in 1972 and finally Chairman of the business in 1982 — a role he would perform until his retirement in 1992.

1947

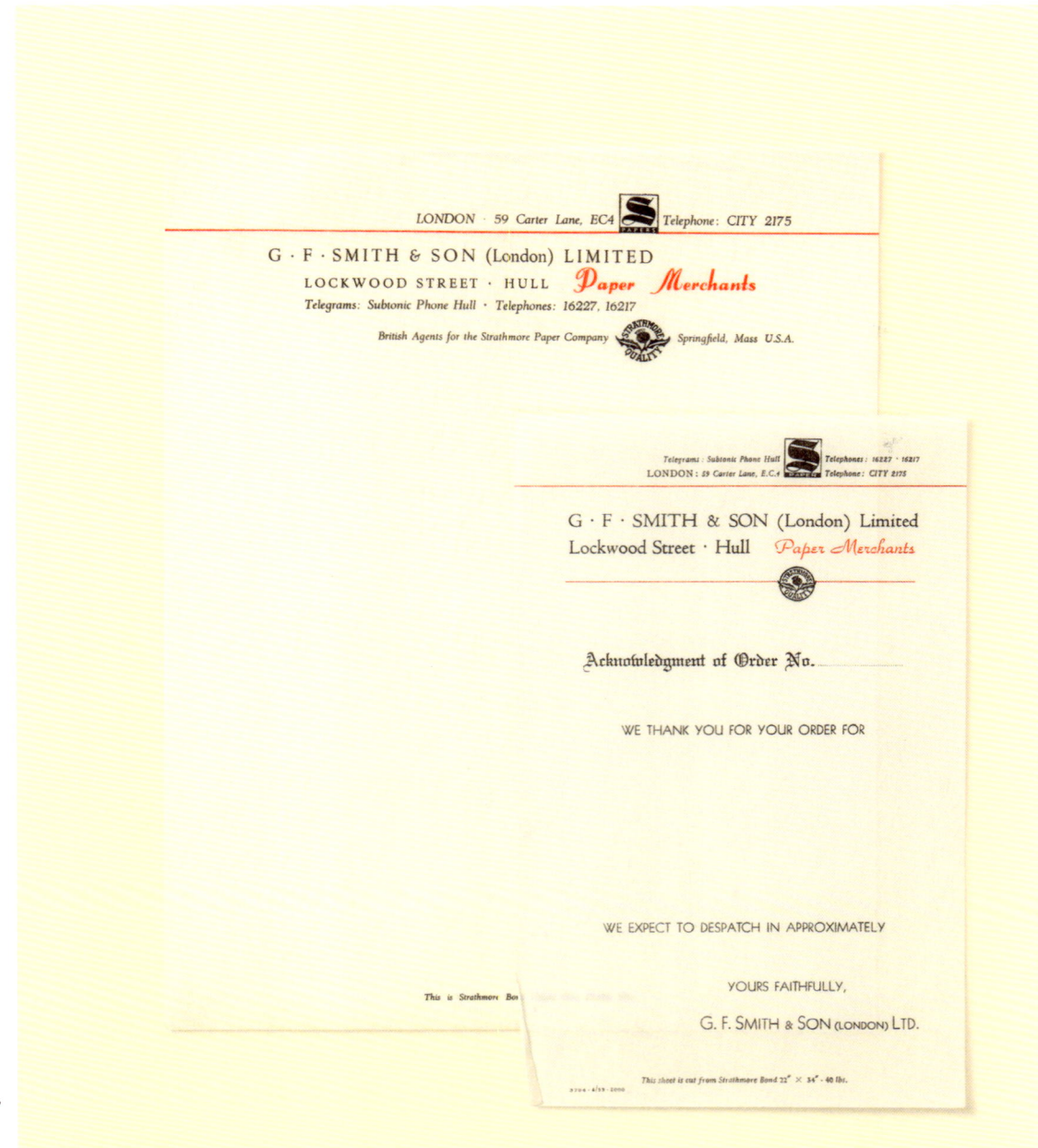

New Beginnings on Lockwood Street, Hull

With the war over, the demand for commercial printing papers rises dramatically. G.F Smith has to find new premises from which it can rebuild the business.

The company purchases a three-story building on Lockwood Street in Hull for £5,000. It had been used as a munitions factory and needs significant renovation before being occupied. A shortage in building supplies means a significant amount of recycled material is used in the construction work. When the company takes possession of the building they find a mountain of wooden rifle butts left by the previous occupants. The building contractor uses them to make beautiful parquet tiles for the offices, some of which can still be seen today.

New buildings are added including a single-storey factory and a two-storey extension with a powerhouse, canteen and kitchen. New equipment including embossers, pasting machines and guillotines is installed and the work is completed in 1947.

Food and a Sense of Community

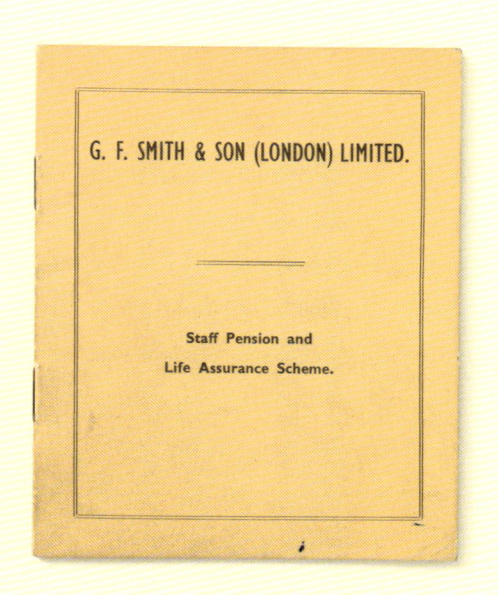

Though food is still rationed, the government makes additional supplies available to any business that provides meals to its staff. To promote well-being, Mr Thomlinson uses the canteen to ensure staff will enjoy a nutritious hot meal during the working day at a reduced cost. The canteen serves a two-course meal and a hot drink for one and sixpence a day (equivalent to seven and a half pence today). Junior members of staff pay just a shilling (equivalent to five pence today). Even as late as the early 2000s when the canteen was closed due to a lack of demand the company still charged just seven and half pence for a meal.

Safeguarding Retirement

New premises in Hull and London mean an increase in staff numbers as the business gears up for growth. The company introduces the G. F Smith & Son (London) Limited pension scheme for all employees as a means of helping those approaching retirement and as an incentive to new recruits.

1950s

A Lifetime of Loyalty

Photographs from the archives show (top) women in the workshop; (bottom) junior members of the Hull sales office, Jack Matthews (left) and John Alexander (right). John becomes a Director of the company in 1968 and then serves as Managing Director from 1982 to 1994 before assuming the role of Chairman from 1992 to 2005.

G.F Smith's coloured and textured papers produce wonderful results when used with a wide range of print processes. The increasing use of lithography and the introduction of small offset printing grows the popularity of many of the company's ranges.

1953

Release of the Coronation Covers Promotion

Mr Thomlinson celebrates the Queen's Coronation by producing a new cover range offering a collection of red, white and blue colours, in a selection of embossing textures with matching envelopes. The Coronation Covers promotion is received by every contact registered on the company's mailing list. Though greatly expanded and improved, the mailing list is still based on the work of Miss Harrison back in 1916.

17/10/1958

we shall only know in the light of future experience of the hours we require you to work.

All Bank Holidays are normally paid in full, also two weeks holiday per annum, and we shall apply this same pro-rata basis in computing the amounts to which you are entitled. With regard to holiday dates, as far as possible you will be allowed to make your own arrangements, but you will appreciate that these must be fixed at the convenience of the company and also to fit in with the arrangements of the senior members of the staff. We do stipulate that the two holiday weeks should be taken together.

To terminate this contract of service it is understood that either side will give the other one weeks notice in writing to end on a Friday.

As you know, the possibility is envisaged of transferring you to our full time staff list next February or March; should this happen any special arrangements mentioned above because of your being a part-time worker will be automatically superseded so that you will then be on exactly the same basis as the rest of our staff.

Will you please carefully read through the above details and confirm in writing your acceptance of the position offered, by signing and returning to me the enclosed letter.

Yours faithfully,
G. F. Smith & Son (London) Ltd.

G. E. Southern,
Secretary.

PS. I am arranging to send you some of our literature as I thought you may care to have a glance through this in order to obtain a first acquaintance with some of our lines and some of the terms used in this trade, as you will no doubt find this very helpful to you when you commence with us.

GES/VH

1958

Handling Paperwork

The paperwork above is sent to applicants for the position of shorthand typist. Each undertakes a shorthand and typing exam at interview.

Published in Penrose

The piece above is the first promotional insert that G.F Smith includes in the Penrose Annual. The Annual features articles and advertorials promoting many of Britain's major paper, print and design companies. G.F Smith will support this publication over many decades, producing iconic sample books that display stunning combinations of ink on paper. The insert shown here displays all the company's range names in display typefaces of the period.

Photographed on Colorplan Pale Grey from G.F Smith

1963

G.F Smith Regains its Independence

Mr Thomlinson, along with Cyril Stephenson, Peter Frank and Ted Southern set about raising the capital to enable the company to regain its independence after 40 years of American ownership. Hammermill Corporation of America, the new owners of Strathmore Paper Mill, undertakes and completes the sale of G.F Smith back to its management team.

The Board of Directors, now in full control of the company, identifies four market opportunities to offer G.F Smith new growth potential. First, there is the company's independence. Second, there is the impact of the litho printing revolution. Third, the growth and impact of colour communications is by now overwhelming. And finally, the influence of graphic design on print and paper specification is already profound. Promotional budgets are spent educating and inspiring the use of coloured and textured paper; the emerging graphic design community is the principal target.

1964

Release of the Cover Print Media Sample Book

With the introduction of colour television and the new power of colour as an advertising tool, G.F Smith's range of coloured paper is being utilised in new and exciting ways.

The Cover Print Media sample book is designed to be an educational tool demonstrating the performance of G.F Smith's covers when printed using litho, letterpress, silkscreen and foiling processes. This publication offers guidance on how to attain the best results and includes printed acetate roamer sheets to aid print colour specification along with a colour selector to show all the available products.

1965

Designers Choice

The first graphic design courses are introduced into art colleges. A steady stream of graduates become the first to establish new and vibrant graphic design businesses. This development also leads to designers taking greater individual control of print and paper specification, and places a responsibility on suppliers to help educate and inspire this new and ambitious audience.

Information Graphics

Bill Mackay is appointed design consultant to help build a strong company identity and produce the sample books and promotional collateral. The partnership will last more than 40 years. With Bill Mackay's help, new promotional material encourages the use of G.F Smith's papers by focusing on demonstration and education showing how the papers perform with existing and new printing technologies.

The above photo shows Bill Mackay (left), Neil Pack (Hull Sales Clerk, who later became a London Director), Ron Jackson (Sales Office Manager) and Doris Coe (Hull Sales Clerk).

1966

Pushing Print Boundaries

The Coverful Boards promotion was a series of eight bi-monthly communications using different stocks, messages and images to show the print potential of G.F Smith papers.

The Directors give Peter Frank the responsibility for directing all sales and marketing activity and provide him with an annual promotional budget that allows him to work with Bill Mackay. The first change Mackay and his team make is to change the company logo for a more decorative single 'S' symbol, reversed out of a solid circle.

1967

Release of The Elements Promotion

A series of four promotional mailers produced by Bill Mackay,
these iconic promotions are designed to educate and
encourage both designers and printers to print colour on colour.
The piece lifts G.F Smith's profile thanks to strong imagery,
an exceptional standard of printing and crisply written copy.

1968

Colour Trends

Bill Mackay's growing knowledge of the graphic, fashion and print sectors becomes a real asset. Seeing the move to stronger and brighter colours, he develops a new paper range called 'Plan 8'. These eight fashionable colours were very new to paper and board ranges across the industry. Success is immediate, and the range becomes the forerunner to the development of Colorplan.

The End of an Era

After 63 years of loyal service, 53 of which were spent as a Director, the company mourns the death of Mr Thomlinson.

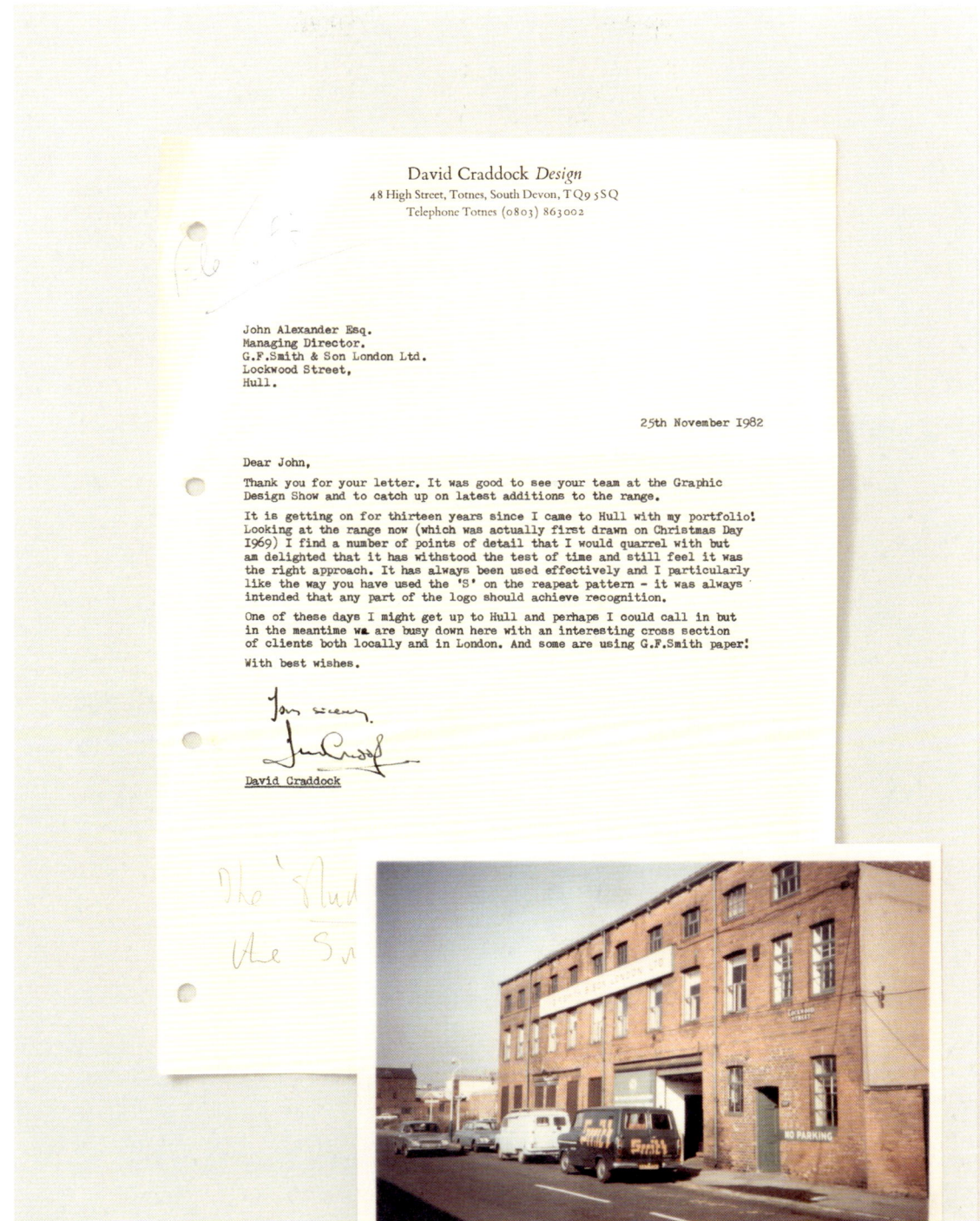

> **David Craddock** *Design*
> 48 High Street, Totnes, South Devon, TQ9 5SQ
> Telephone Totnes (0803) 863002
>
> John Alexander Esq.
> Managing Director.
> G.F.Smith & Son London Ltd.
> Lockwood Street,
> Hull.
>
> 25th November 1982
>
> Dear John,
>
> Thank you for your letter. It was good to see your team at the Graphic Design Show and to catch up on latest additions to the range.
>
> It is getting on for thirteen years since I came to Hull with my portfolio! Looking at the range now (which was actually first drawn on Christmas Day 1969) I find a number of points of detail that I would quarrel with but am delighted that it has withstood the test of time and still feel it was the right approach. It has always been used effectively and I particularly like the way you have used the 'S' on the reapeat pattern – it was always intended that any part of the logo should achieve recognition.
>
> One of these days I might get up to Hull and perhaps I could call in but in the meantime we are busy down here with an interesting cross section of clients both locally and in London. And some are using G.F.Smith paper!
>
> With best wishes.
>
> David Craddock

1969

A New Identity

Students at the London College of Printing are set a design brief as part of their course to produce a corporate identity for the company. The work of David Craddock is so exceptional that the Board immediately purchases it from him. Bill Mackay then incorporates the new logo into all the company's stationery, sample books and promotions. Craddock stays in regular contact with the company, and as is shown in the letter above, continues to take great pride in the work that he now sees used across all of the company's communications.

Signs of Change

The photograph above shows the Lockwood Street premises in Hull. The new company logo can be seen on the van. Today, visitors will notice that very little has changed (other than the signage boards) since the building was first occupied in 1947.

Portrait of a Company

Photographed on Colorplan Vellum White from G.F Smith

1972

The Launch of Colorplan

The success of the 'Plan 8' range sees the company rationalise the entire product portfolio. Working with Bill Mackay, John Alexander talks extensively with customers and reviews sales of G.F Smith's ranges and colours. The rationalisation is completed in 1971, and in 1972 the result is called 'Colour Programme'. Ready for sale, the new range of 40 colours contains existing and many newly created colours. It is launched as Colorplan.

A New World of Colour

The image above shows the Colour Programme Selector, launched in 1972. Not only is it the first time that G.F Smith uses the 'chip' style of presentation to allow for easy review and selection of a broad range of colour papers, it is the first time any company in the industry uses this now familiar method. Still in use by G.F Smith today, it was soon to be adopted by the majority of the competition.

1973

Paper Partnerships

G.F Smith begins an important partnership with James Cropper Speciality Papers. Over several stages of development and under the close direction of G.F Smith, Croppers strives to meet the impeccable standards they have been set. As a result of their dedication to excellence in paper manufacture, Croppers becomes the mill responsible for the production of Colorplan. They remain one of the company's most valued partners.

More Visibility for Colorplan

To make new print and design contacts, G.F Smith attends its first trade exhibition at Nor-print in Leeds. The stand is created to promote the recently launched Colour Programme, which included Colorplan. The stand highlights many of the strong colours available, supported by displays of commercially printed examples. The success of this first venture into trade exhibitions sees G.F Smith regularly taking a stand at major trade shows.

New Managers Help Grow Sales

Having joined the company in 1961, Neil Haslam becomes the Director of the London office in 1973. Neil eventually becomes Joint Managing Director with Richard Bolton in 1994. Along with the general development and growth of the business, the pair had already been instrumental in the early stages of development of the now enormously successful Colour Programme. Richard Bolton becomes sole Managing Director in 1997.

1979

More Orders Means More Space

A new warehouse is opened to help manage the growth in business the company has been enjoying over the early part of the 1970s. To maximise capacity, one third of the floor area at the rear of the building is fitted with an electronically powered moveable racking system mounted on tracks, allowing for fork lift access to the sides opened by the operator. The system generated an additional 40% of storage capability primarily used as bulk storage for products. The rest of the warehouse was racked out with standard pallets holding just a few thousand sheets of each stock item for ease of hand-picking. The Directors make the decision on this system, the first of its kind in the paper industry, after visiting a power station on the recommendation of their architects.

Standing second from the right in the top photo is Peter Frank. From his original job as office boy he would spend the rest of his working life with the company, finally retiring from the position of Chairman in 1992.

Specialised Salespeople

Anne Beytell becomes the company's first Graphic Arts Paper Consultant. Based in the London office, her role is to help create awareness of G. F Smith's papers and boards among the growing numbers of graphic design businesses in central London.
The post was in addition to a dozen or so Paper Consultants already employed by the company and who spent time with the widest possible range of customers including printers, merchants, end users, designers and art colleges.

Photographed on Marlmarque Marble White from G.F Smith

1980s

Samples in the Selector

From the beginning of the decade the 'Selector' becomes a primary sales tool. The frequent introduction of new ranges means a new version of the selector is produced every two years and sent out to the entire mailing list. These easy to use sample books are ideal for the company's own growing sales team and allow customers to make easier decisions on which papers to specify. As the business grows, the sales team meets regularly to discuss customer feedback, new papers and how to stay ahead of the competition.

1985

Photographic Memories

Photographic from G.F Smith is established to offer and service the professional photographer with bespoke photo albums and photographic mounts and folders.

1995

New Services Recognise Market Demand

To meet the changing needs of customers, and maximise the opportunities presented by new market sectors within the paper, print and graphical industries the company introduces new services including Luxury Packaging, Greetings Cards, Export, Retail and Digital.

1998

Rankin Changes the Game

A promotion produced in collaboration with photographer Rankin is probably the most important piece of marketing G.F Smith produces in the 1990s. Iconic, bold and unashamedly contemporary, it is the central element in the campaign to launch a new smooth white uncoated paper called Accent Smooth, developed in Britain to meet emerging market demands. The promotion and the paper are instrumental in the growth of the business over the next ten years.

1996

Celebrating British Design

After the ground-breaking work done by Bill Mackay, G.F Smith sets off in a new design direction and commissions SEA Design. Over the next decade this partnership builds an iconic brand and inspires a generation of designers.

Photographed on Gmund Bier Wiezen from G.F Smith

2005

Celebrating Creativity

The relationship with SEA continues with three sample book collections, each using a different 'ink cloud' theme. SEA is commissioned to produce a series of print promotions on Naturalis from G.F Smith featuring the creative work of Peter Blake and Wim Crouwel among others.

2008

Ready for Digital

To meet the increasing demand for papers and boards suitable for digital printing, G.F Smith introduces a Sapphire Coating Press to enable the company to offer their digital collection as a next day service. The promotion that supports this new offering is called 'Print Test'.

2010

A New Approach to Paper Selection

The new Selector, designed by SEA, intends to more accurately reflect the way that designers go about the task of choosing paper. For some, colour is the primary concern, before considerations of material, texture and weight. But, occasionally, the process is reversed, making style the most important factor. The set offered three modes of paper selection, by colour, black and white, or range.

2012

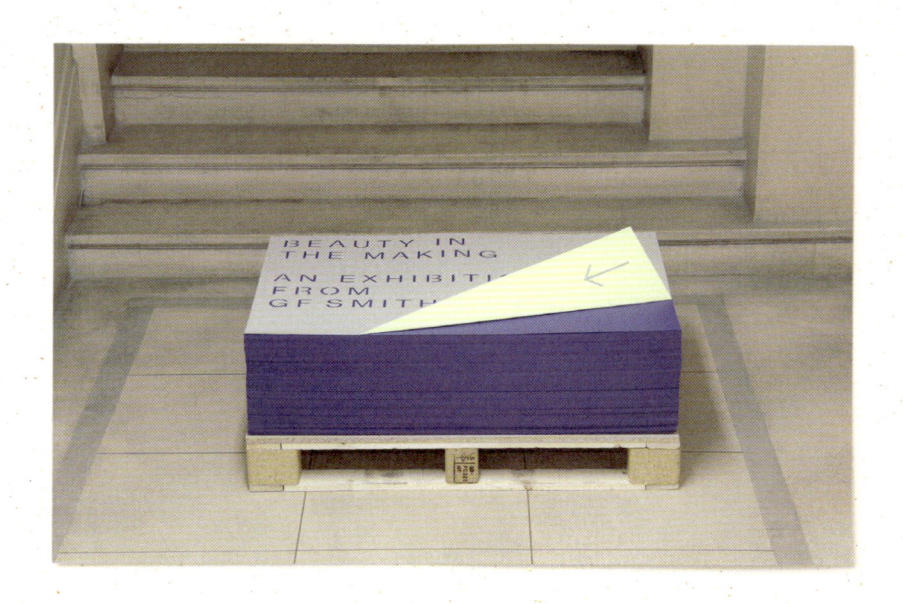

Craft and Creativity

Continuing the theme of educating and inspiring paper users that began in the 1960s, G.F Smith partners with the British Council, Monotype London and It's Nice That to stage 'Beauty in the Making'. A free event held over five days, and the first work commissioned from branding and design consultancy Made Thought, the show is a celebration of the hidden skills and craftsmanship that lie behind the scenes of the creative industry. The manufacture and application of paper is central to the exhibition's subject matter.

G.F Smith begins to work with design agency Studio Makgill on a series of promotions for Naturalis paper and materials to support the launch of the Fine Coated range. They also work on a new swatch book for Greetings from G.F Smith, and the development of materials for Photographic from G.F Smith.

2014 Onwards

2014 begins with the unveiling of a new visual identity and design direction. The work — spanning print and digital communications — is intended to better reflect the legacy, stature and future ambitions of the company.

These ambitions include the continued development and global expansion of Colorplan, adding new chapters to what already stands as a great British success story. With a distinct identity and a concerted marketing and sales push, the range is seeing growth in exports to new markets including Australia, China, Germany and America.

And it is perhaps no coincidence that in a year where we will reflect on our legacy and stature, and drive forward our ambitions, that we will also celebrate the importance of our people.
In 2014, we will recognise the fact that 36 members of the team have given more than 20 years of service to the company.

Our continued success is due, in no small part, to their dedication and loyalty.

Our People
―――――――――――――

Phoenixmotion Xantur 150gsm from G.F Smith

Portrait of a Company

Kat

Before I started here I helped run a print shop in Hull, and put myself through college studying graphic design and as students we all knew G.F Smith very well. At the print shop I started specifying G.F Smith papers, and I just knew I wanted to work here, and so when a job came up, I just went for it. I work on The Paper Smith, which helps people get smaller amounts of our paper, like start up businesses and individuals in the craft industry.

I also do a lot of paper crafting. I made a rotating carousel, with horses, all out of G.F Smith paper. When I got married I spent my spare time making everything I could from buttonholes to invitations to place settings and cages with little birds in them, all from our paper. Well, I had to because I'd invited colleagues. I would go home, cut out hundreds of flowers, and make sure they were all perfect. I can bend paper, stretch it, warm it up with a hairdryer and cool it down and make things that you couldn't do from just folding. I'm not good at origami. But if I see something I can remake it in paper. I guess I'm a paper manipulator. It's more artistic and it's about paper's texture, and about making something real.

The Paper Smith from G.F Smith (7 years)

Photographed against Colorplan Cobalt from G.F Smith

Portrait of a Company

Mark

I trained as a fine artist, painted for a while, then worked in an art materials shop and became a picture framer, so I already had a strong sense of colour and a solid understanding of paper and craft.

When I started work in the paper trade, before joining G.F Smith, I was taught to sell in a very particular way. It involved talking about the sample paper or book that I had in my hands and holding onto it for as long as humanly possible. By the end of my well-rehearsed pitch, I felt less like someone who loved paper and more like a salesman, and the customer had all but lost interest. It was pretty frustrating.

There are two big differences with how I work at G.F Smith. First, I don't sell. I have a conversation with the designers, printers and creative people that I meet. And second, I don't keep hold of the paper. For designers, it's a lot to do with texture so why would I deny them the opportunity to get their hands on the wonderful things we have in our Collection?

The reaction I most enjoy is when people see a new paper or new sample book, and smile, and reach across the table. That's what happens when you have the finest papers and a reputation for beautiful and inspiring communications.

Paper Consultant, South-West England (9 years)

Photographed against Colorplan Smoke from G.F Smith

Portrait of a Company

Dan

I took an NVQ and then a City & Guilds through Hull City council. During the course I went on a placement to a local print finishers. I was accepted to do a two-year apprenticeship with them. They took me on at the end of it, and I worked there until Photographic from G.F Smith took us under their wing.

The company moved from its original site, and brought the machinery we had there, including eight Heidelberg letterpresses that we still use as part of our daily work. These machines were all but finished in the print sector as a whole. There's the odd one or two kicking around but I don't know of anywhere with the number of Heidelberg's that we have, with the number of staff we have who are trained up and have the depth of knowledge to be able to use them like we do to make the best of the machine's capabilities. If they were all ticking over for a full working day, we could produce 56,000 items a day, foiling or cutting or more. It's a fantastic sight.

Production Team Leader (18 years)

Photographed against Colorplan Real Grey from G.F Smith

Portrait of a Company

I started at G.F Smith, working on the blocking machines. Now, I'm a member of the Make Book team. We check every book that passes through here. We have to count them, check the foil blocking, check the title or name that's been embossed, and make sure everything is absolutely perfect with the order before we can let it go. If something's been framed, we check the frame and the glass. We're the final stage before orders leave the warehouse so our job is to make sure that what the customer gets is what the customer expects and in perfect condition.

We all rely on each other to make sure the process works smoothly, which is why the whole team takes pride in what it does.

Make Book from G.F Smith (6 years)

Sarah

Photographed against Colorplan Bespoke Colour from G.F Smith

Portrait of a Company

Issak

I've been with G.F Smith since 2003. I joined as a driver — the job that I still do today. My day, which is spent delivering the paper to the customer, starts about 8 o'clock in the morning. The paper has already arrived from Hull via Leicester about two hours earlier. I load up my van, last order first, and I make up to 20 deliveries a day making sure I am on time so that the customers stay happy. I take great care of my van because I'm always in it. I don't fill up the dashboard with papers, wrappers and cans. It's very tidy.

Before I came to G.F Smith I worked with an automobile recovery service and I learned so much from those days about getting around London. And before that I made deliveries for a bakery — but my wife asked me to stop bringing cakes home every day.

This job makes me very happy. I know most of the customers now, and they're very good people. They've got my number so if they need me, they can call, and I can tell them exactly when I will be there. I'll start out with a cup of tea at the office, and I probably have four cups of tea a day when I am on my deliveries. If I finish early I get back to the warehouse and help out there. After that, I have half an hour at the gym, every day, and then I get home and see my kids.

Driver, London (10 years)

Photographed against Colorplan Cobalt from G.F Smith

Portrait of a Company

Adam

I remember the first time I came here was for my interview, and I didn't know where I was going. There was a little bell on the side of one of the doors and just as I was about to ring it one of the warehouse guys walked over and said "Hello there, who are you looking for? Is there anything I can do to help you?" That was great, and from just meeting that one person I soon saw that everyone was like that and made me feel welcome. Everyone shares a feeling of pride in doing a good job.

Warehouse Operative (4 years)

Photographed against Colorplan Real Grey from G.F Smith

Portrait of a Company

Aimee

My grandmother, Nanny Eve, worked at G.F Smith for more than 20 years. She would answer the telephones, handle the orders that came in and then type them out on her typewriter, checking and double checking that the details were all correct.

Every now and then when I was a kid, I would visit her at the old London office. I remember that when she had typed up the orders or sample requests she would roll them up and drop them through a hole not far from her desk that would go straight to the warehouse. I loved the idea of that.

Many years later I was fortunate enough to get an interview to work at the company, and thrilled to get the job. Apart from doing a lot of the things that my Nanny Eve did, I spend quite a bit of time looking after the students that frequently visit the offices with questions about paper. And Nanny Eve still loves to hear the stories from work, and she still joins all the other fellow retirees every year at the G.F Smith retiree dinner.

Sales, London (2 years)

Photographed against Colorplan Cobalt from G.F Smith

Portrait of a Company

When I first started at G.F Smith I was wrapping and dispatching paper orders. Now, I work on the cutting and embossing machines.

Back home, I went through printing school and then worked for six years at a web-offset printers where the paper came off huge rolls. The paper I work with now is much more exclusive and more valuable. If I'm cutting, we get the paper and the dimensions, and I make sure it is trimmed exactly. And embossing is like printing, just without the ink.

I like it here, because whatever sort of day I have had, there is always a sense of family.

Cutter and Embosser (3 years)

Arturs

Photographed against Colorplan Bespoke Colour from G.F Smith

Portrait of a Company

When you're surrounded by paper all day, one of the things I think about is what the paper might be turned into, and where's it going to go. And every now and again you'll see something and be able to say 'I drew that paper'. It could be a box for perfume, or boxes for whisky. You'll see different products laid out in front of you, and it will be our brand of paper, and you'll think of the team, and take pride in the role you played in it.

Fork Lift, Stock Management, Distribution (27 years)

Tony
___

Photographed against Colorplan Dark Grey from G.F Smith

Portrait of a Company

I'm passionate about paper. I once considered leaving the paper industry unless I could work for G.F Smith because I thought they were the most innovative paper company in the UK.
So I'm thrilled to be here.

I really enjoy working with designers and brands because they are always passionate about paper and our paper in particular, to the extent that we've developed something of a cult following. Designers always want to see me, even if they're snowed under with work, and their reaction to what we offer them is always inspiring. When they've done their work, I get called back in to take a sample of what was finally printed and so I get to see what they did with our paper. As a result I've got a vast amount of printed samples that I keep because I know a lot of love and care has gone into the design and production of it. I use these samples to help inspire other designers so they can see what is possible with our papers.

Paper Consultant, London (1 year)

Rachael

Photographed against Colorplan Bespoke Colour from G.F Smith

Portrait of a Company

I drive a lorry and make deliveries within a 10-mile radius of Hull. I start at 8.30am. I'll get in, get my delivery list and I'm off. Each set of deliveries takes a couple of hours, so I'm back to the warehouse about four times a day.

The business was a quarter of the size when I was hired. In truth I should have retired a couple of years ago, but I think it would do me in, and I've got a young son now, and I feel fit. I was playing rugby league till I was 55-years old. I would play football in the morning, then watch a game or two, and then go to rugby training and I'd feel guilty because I didn't have a single ache the following day.

A few years back, one of the lads here said he'd won a lot of cups at running, and there's a yard here, about 100 yards from fence to fence, so we thought we'd have a go. I shouted start, and I was a yard in front of him before he'd even moved. "False start!" he said. So we got someone else to shout start. I gave him a yard and finished a yard ahead of him. Imagine being beaten by a 56-year old.

Driver, Hull (34 years)

Melvyn

Photographed against Colorplan Cobalt from G.F Smith

Portrait of a Company

To all our staff and Directors both past and present,
a sincere thank you for your commitment, passion and energy.

Our Work

Portrait of a Company

Colorplan Powder Green 135 gsm from G.F Smith

A Founding Legacy

George Frederick Smith was a man with a singular passion for paper. Both he and his son were driven by a belief in its beauty and possibilities and shared an admiration for the craft of the printers and publishers that used it. In 1885 George founded G.F Smith & Son as a paper merchant. It was his vision and ambition that steered the company through challenging times; his belief in the business saw him expand its horizons.

George travelled with an almost obsessive energy, by land and sea, to seek out the very finest paper manufacturers of their day. From an office in London and a warehouse within a stone's throw of the docks on the Humber in Hull, he won business in Europe, found partners in America and gathered a loyal and industrious staff. G.F Smith was a merchant company in the truest sense.

Nearly 130 years later in a very different world, George Frederick Smith's fortitude and determination are qualities we are proud to carry forward. He was a driven, hardworking man, loyal to and respected by those who worked for him and those who bought his paper. He was responsible in the way he ran his business. He was curious enough to search out the finest paper he could find wherever it was, and determined enough to find a way of bringing it back.

Above all else, George Frederick Smith was celebrated for his passion for paper, and if our predecessor left just one thing we are proud to embody it is this. Paper defined his era, and despite much evidence to the contrary, it defines ours. The world might have changed; our love of paper and its possibilities has not.

George Frederick Smith

Born in 1832, George Frederick Smith entered Vi[ctorian Britain] at the peak of the Industrial Revolution, a countr[y of] change and progress. He started professional life [as an] apprentice in Grantham before making his way th[rough the length] and breadth of Britain as a commercial traveller, [selling paper] and stationery to printers and publishers. He ma[rried] and as his family grew, he looked to capitalise on his experiences in the paper trade as a means of securing their financial future and to create employment for his children. So, in 1885, George Frederick Smith founded G.F Smith & Son, establishing an office in London and entrusting his son Thomas Brooks Smith to build the business in Hull.

Make Book from G.F Smith

Make Book is a way to create one-off books, to your design, finished to an incredibly high standard of production. Hand assembled in Hull, each book is printed using a photographic process and silver halide technology onto professional archive quality paper. You can choose from 50 Colorplan colours as a cover or endpaper, and can have a foil blocked or debossed cover. Make Book is available in three sizes (B5, A4 and A3) and can run from as few as eight pages to a maximum of 100 and thanks to the lay flat binding, your design can run right across the spine, from corner to corner. View the options at gfsmith.com/makebook.

Brand as Custodian

As the proud custodians of George Frederick Smith's legacy, we have two driving passions. First, we remain dedicated to preserving and maintaining the paper collection, adding to and improving it. Second, we are dedicated to the well-being of our staff, safeguarding the knowledge, experience and expertise that they bring, nurtured through training and development and passed from master to apprentice.

We also maintain the company's rich history. We chart its growth, and take account of how it has responded successfully to the huge changes we've seen in the worlds of commercial art and graphic design. Though enemy bombs destroyed much of the company's earliest archives in the Second World War, what remains is carefully protected. There is the very significant task of maintaining some of the remarkable machinery we have on our factory floor, from envelope making machines to the magnificent embossing equipment that has been a fixture of G.F Smith since the 1930s. Thanks to expert care and constant use these incredible machines are still going strong.

Finally, there is the preservation of the pioneering mentality; a desire, indeed an obsession, to seek out, secure and make precious resources available to a demanding audience with an appetite for the new, the different and the most impeccable paper.

Though the role of the custodian might seem to be focused on the past, our own view is that this sense of duty to protect what we have today makes us best placed to be ready for what tomorrow might bring.

G . F SMITH

1885 ONWARDS

The Custodian Mark

Our mark is an acknowledgment of our role as a custodian; protecting what is important to us now, but ensuring that we never lose sight of where we started. We're certainly proud of our beginnings in 1885, and of the path that George Frederick Smith set out upon, and it is why this mark bears his name; every time it appears, it signifies our determination to live up to his standards. His honesty, and the trust and respect in which he was held are values we work hard to maintain.

Equally important is to make sure that what we are creating today is protected with equal care and a sense of history. So when we say that we are a business from '1885 Onwards' it is far from a need to be tied to the past, but an acknowledgment that as a forward looking company, G.F Smith is proud of its history because our people, our collection, our reputation and the knowledge embodied in all of this have all been formed from our experiences across the generations.

Portrait of a Company

People First

___

We care about our people as much as we do our paper simply because nothing we do would be possible without them. Their values of loyalty, trust, hard work and a desire to learn and then pass on skills and experience are the values that continue to underpin our work. A solid business, and the ability and determination to work through significant challenges, has created sustained employment for generations of families in the great tradition of our founder. Apprentices have joined us, and never left. Others with specialist skills have been sought out, brought in and made our own.

It is the knowledge our people hold that allows us to offer the range of highly specialist services that so many of our competitors can't. Each member of our staff already does what they do exceptionally well, but they also want to get better, smarter and more efficient to be ready for the challenges of tomorrow.

Our Services: Paper Consultants

Our Paper Consultants have decades of gathered experience, all of which they're only too happy to place at your disposal. Their passion for paper is limitless, as is their knowledge of what it is capable of, and what G.F Smith can help a designer achieve with it. So, whether it's very early stages on a project, a technical challenge you're facing, or you simply need to be walked through the scope and scale of our Collection, an informal chat with one of our Paper Consultants will be the perfect way to start.

G . F
SMITH
1885 ONWARDS

It is the fact that our Paper Consultants don't just know our Collection and technical abilities like the back of their hand (and love any opportunity they get to talk about it), but that they are equally accomplished at listening and responding to the changing needs of their customers. And it is the fact that the leadership of the business and a succession of astute, ambitious and conscientious Directors reserve as much admiration for the people who make G.F Smith tick as they do for the papers that the business is renowned for.

People are, and will always remain, the fabric of G.F Smith.

A British Signature

We are proud of our British heritage, and, like many of the design companies we work with, proud too of our independence. An involvement with other great British creative enterprises, like Stella McCartney and Monotype London re-affirms the fact that British ingenuity is alive, well, and thriving.

In part, our sense of Britishness is about backbone. When our predecessors had to rebuild, brick by brick, after the bombs fell upon Hull in 1941, it was a demonstration not only of the fabled British stiff upper lip but also of a resilience borne of the perils and privations of conflict. This spirit further strengthened our resolute determination to sustain the business in its home of Hull and from our London offices too. When the business began to expand, and our paper collections were in demand and in use all over the world, we flew the flag with immense pride, acknowledging not just our own success, but what our success said about British industry.

As a result of a continued pioneering spirit, our connections and friendships are truly international. But we'll never forget our roots. It is fitting then that our own typeface, designed in Britain, is a celebration of a particularly British aesthetic and print traditions to which we have been bound since the founding of the business; it conveys a sense of Britishness in every word we write.

G .
g M
7

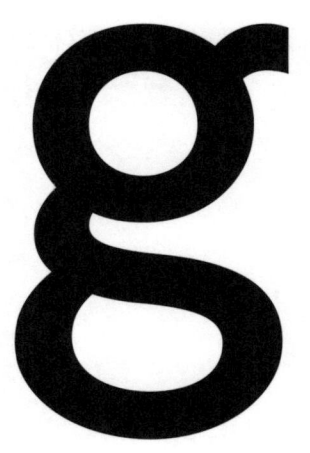

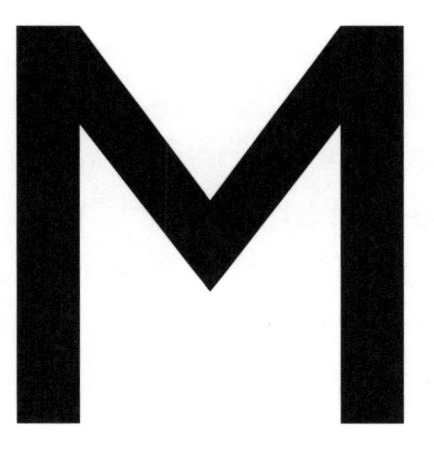

A Typeface of Man and Machine

The early part of the 20th century saw the dawn of the machine age. Companies were born, industries were formed, and a new family of typefaces emerged to respond to this revolution in the means of production. Less austere than the sans serifs that originated in Germany, but clearly still unrelated to the predominant serif style of the day, these became known as humanist sans, where shapes and outlines were melded from the mechanised and the handcrafted. It is in the same spirit that we have created our own typeface, G.F Smith, a conscious balance of machine and calligraphy and a powerful acknowledgment of our roots.

Portrait of a Company

Curated Collection

George Frederick Smith was a curator in the traditional sense. It was his obsession and passion to travel the world in search of paper and forge long-lasting relationships with the people who manufactured it. Today, this aspect of his earliest endeavours is at the core of our business, inherent in everything we do.

For us, curation is not a fad, nor is it a process that can be mechanised. The products we find and supply are measured by their tactility, texture and touch. Whether it's a unique embossing or a particular weight, the hand is a fundamental tool of our trade. The hand allows us to feel, sense and judge, to compare, dismiss or accept, and ultimately, to select. We look for qualities not immediately obvious to the naked eye, papers with a special, sometimes unique purpose. We get answers to the questions we know we will be asked. And even when a paper steals our hearts (which they do on a regular basis), we have to establish that there will be a regularity of supply and a guarantee of consistent quality.

We shy away from gimmicks and look for future classics. This is what we do in order to bring the finest available products to the market, striking a careful balance between aesthetic and practical needs. This is what George Frederick Smith did nearly 130 years or more ago, and it is what continues to set us apart today.

The Collection from G.F Smith

Our Collection might not be the largest by number in the industry, but it is without question the most carefully and consciously assembled. Our ranges are divided across six distinct categories: Colorplan, Fine Uncoated, Fine Coated, Textured, Specialist and Digital Papers. We choose paper for very specific reasons. It must perform to the highest standards of printing, whether in litho and digital processes and be practical and malleable. Most importantly, it must be beautiful. With an eye on the future, the Collection also includes some of the world's most innovative substrates. View our Collection at gsmith.com/thecollection.

Portrait of a Company

Heart of the Company

Thanks to specialist equipment and the skills we've developed and protected over generations, G.F Smith can offer paper products, bespoke makings and highly tailored services specifically developed to meet the needs of the creative industries. We offer a degree of craft, customisation and flexibility that is almost impossible to replicate.

In part it's about machinery, but in the main it's about the abilities of our team. The exceptional skills of our master bookbinder means we are able to prepare the most exquisite handmade dummies, from any of our stocks and in a range of bindings and finishes. We can supply envelopes that are machine made or cut, folded, glued and finished by hand, at sizes from business card to A3 and at every possible measurement in-between, in any of the papers in our Collection. We can produce bespoke makings, with papers tailored to your specific requirements at a specific size and weight, and, if you require it, of a unique signature colour. And, since the advent of digital printing, we have tested and developed coatings that allow us to prepare any of our stocks for digital printing.

Colorplan from G.F Smith

Colorplan's current collection is the result of careful curation, based on an understanding of the needs of our customers. It is designed for print and packaging to the very highest standards, and is truly comprehensive, comprised of 50 colours, 25 embossing textures and 8 weights (from 100gsm to 700gsm). It is guaranteed for digital printing, is FSC accredited and fade resistant. It can be made to a bespoke size and weight with a minimum order of one tonne (equates to only 6,000 A1 sheets of 270gsm) and in a unique colour above orders of two tonnes. Available as hand-made envelopes from business card to A3 and at every possible measurement in-between, Colorplan can be duplexed six sheets deep to a weight of 700gsm.

Colorplan
Citrine
135gsm
from G.F Smith

From day one Colorplan changed the landscape of printed communications. In the hands of a flourishing generation of graphic designers and forward thinking printers, the range formed the basis of design and advertising work of a style that had simply not been previously possible. Since establishing new levels of colour sophistication and subtle texture, Colorplan has continued to evolve; its range has never been as comprehensive or more ideally suited to meet the demands of the modern creative as it is today.

Born into a changing world, Colorplan remains an iconic and indispensible element of the designer's craft.
In 1972, the revolutionary Colorplan had no predecessor.
Today, it remains without equal.

Portrait of a Company

A Creative Viewpoint

Since the earliest days of the company, we have worked hand in hand with publishers, designers and creative businesses, understanding their needs and acting as a partner in the creation of their work. From printers and academic publishers, through the dawn of commercial art and as suppliers to the first pioneers of British graphic design, we have been on hand to ensure all have had a choice of fine papers to specify and use.

We have a long-held admiration for those who specify our paper, already intrinsically beautiful, and use their own ingenuity and creativity to make it more beautiful still. This admiration takes many forms. From commissioning the design of our own work, to supporting creative organisations like AGI and the Typographic Circle, we acknowledge the unique energy of the creative spirit, and stay true to our own. We are a partner and a provider. We know what we have to do in order to help complete a designer's work. When asked, we will advise. And when pushed, we will always try and find a way. Providing a service that goes beyond duty is what puts us front of mind with our customers.

Celebrating Craft an

G.F Smith is both a
with people we adm
creating our own hig
hosting shows and e
In doing this, we tak
creative community
the British Council a
Making', and since t
The Barbican, the L
Manchester, and Pe
Our commitment is
creative community

Ultimately, what we love to do is work with people as passionate about their work as we are about our own.
It is this instinct that has helped us build a close relationship with the creative community, which we further develop through the instigation and support of creative events.
When these complementary passions meet, it is remarkable what we can create.

Portrait of a Company

Onward Spirit

We're proud to share George Frederick Smith's passion for paper and to be the custodians of his remarkable legacy. This responsibility, to build on our predecessor's achievements, gives us more than a sense of purpose; it's a driving force that binds all our efforts.

We'll continue our obsession with paper, staying curious, looking for new stocks, techniques and innovations. We'll continue to admire and support the spirit and imagination of designers and printers, writers and artists, authors and publishers, and, continue to invest in British creativity to bring our own communications to life. We'll remain fiercely proud of our home city of Hull, and loyal to our next generation of employees, offering them opportunities for growth and stable livelihoods.

Most importantly of all, we'll continue our love affair with paper, and remain in awe of its seemingly limitless capabilities and its inherent beauty and simplicity.
For nearly 130 years, the papers that we've travelled the world to find have brought texture and substance, colour, form and magic to the ideas that are printed upon it.

And so, as we look ahead, we remain true to the legacy of George Frederick Smith, determined to continue to find and supply the very best paper we can in order to inspire the next generation of creative pioneers. It's a vision that connects us to our roots; it's what inspires and drives us forward.

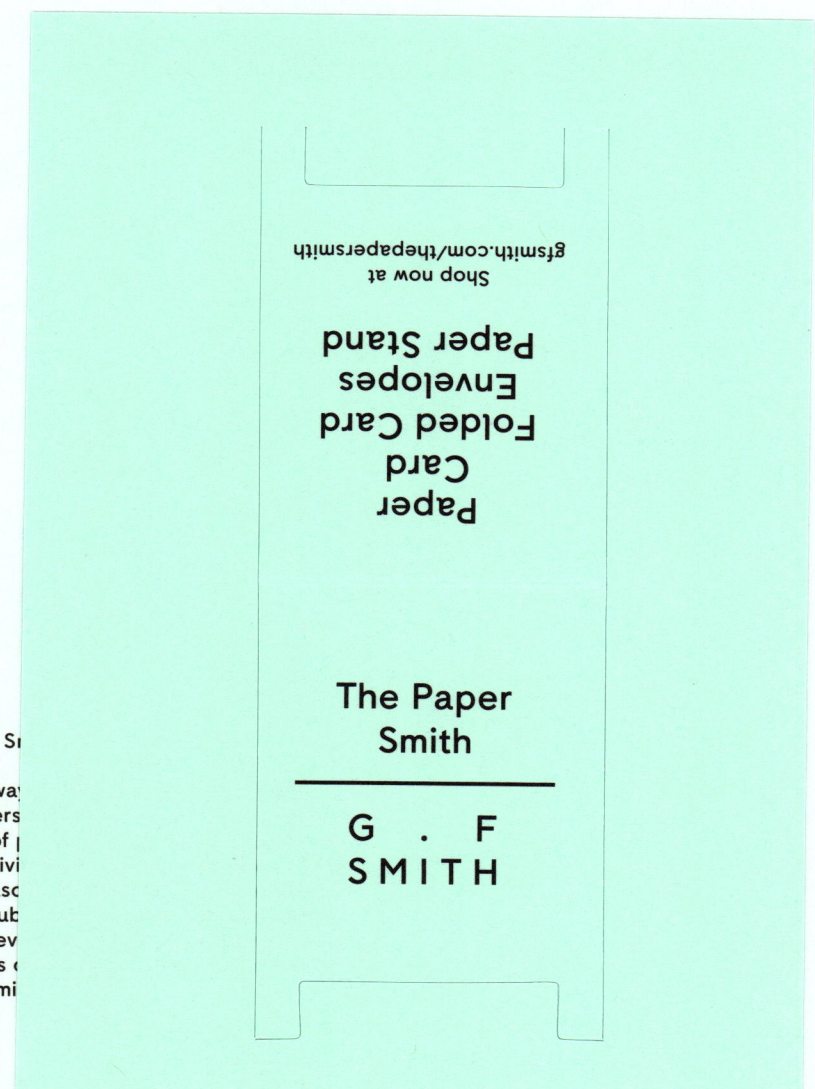

The Paper Smith from G.F S

The Paper Smith is a new wa
from our selection of papers
to buy smaller quantities of
more accessible to the indiv
and themes across the seaso
for new ideas, incredible sub
finishes. The stock will be ev
for designers and devotees
at gfsmith.com/thepapersmi

The Paper Smith

———————

G . F SMITH

Paper
Card
Folded Card
Envelopes
Paper Stand

Shop now at
gfsmith.com/thepapersmith

The Persuasiveness of Quality
Promotion from G.F Smith, 1929

Plike Orange 140gsm from G.F Smith

Portrait of a Company

Quality in printing is not a dilettante indulgence.

It is in fact a necessity of advertising that must pay its way.

The more vital the need of returns from your printed matter, the greater the necessity that it possess the 'persuasiveness of quality'.

Portrait of a Company

You think of your printed matter as so many thousands of pieces to be sent to a 'list' but the list is compiled of individual Jim's and Jack's, or Betty's and Anne's who see but one copy apiece.

They do not know how large an edition you have printed. They do not know that such and such a printer would have done the job for less money.

They do not know, nor do they care, anything at all about the expenses, difficulties or printing problems involved in getting out your printed matter.

Portrait of a Company

They only know that in their hands is a booklet. One booklet.

They are either impressed or unimpressed.

In that one copy is your opportunity.

Make that one copy rise to it.

Portrait of a Company

G.F Smith HULL
Lockwood Street, Hull HU2 0HL
Phone 01482 323 503
Fax 01482 223 174
Email info@gfsmith.com

G.F Smith LONDON
Six Bridges Trading Estate
Marlborough Grove, London SE1 5JT
Phone 020 7394 4660
Fax 020 7394 4661
Email london@gfsmith.com

Published in 2014 by G.F Smith & Son (London) Limited
ISBN 978-0-9928503
Our Story curated by Ray Earle
Our People portrait photography by Toby Coulson
The Collection paper wall photography by GG Archard
Printed in Great Britain
© Copyright G.F Smith
All rights reserved. No part of this publication may be
reproduced or transmitted in any form or by any means,
electronic or mechanical, including photocopy, recording
or any other information storage or retrieval system,
without prior permission in writing from the publisher.

gfsmith.com
gfsmith.com/thecollection
gfsmith.com/thepapersmith
gfsmith.com/makebook

@gfsmithpapers
@colorplanpapers

Colorplan
Turquoise
135 gsm
from G.F Smith